Looking at
Animals

Barbara Taylor • Katy Sleight

Kingfisher Books

About this book

Very young children learn facts more readily when they can join in, so this book contains specially designed activities that allow for plenty of involvement.

Some activities reinforce the fun of learning by asking children to compare pictures and spot the similarities and differences. Some activities teach essential early learning skills such as the concepts of number, shape and colour.

You can extend these activities, for example, by looking for colours on other pages. You can also help by listening enthusiastically to how children talk about the pictures, and by relating them to a child's own experience. Joining in will help children to learn and will make learning fun.

Contents

❧ Animal favourites

I like
birds that fly
in the sky,

and dolphins
that swim
in the sea.

I like camels
that walk
in the sand,

and monkeys that swing
in the trees.

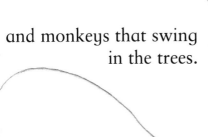

I like
polar bears
that crunch
through the
snow,

and worms that
burrow in the soil.

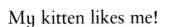

My kitten likes me!

Which animals
do you like best?

🐾 Animal colours

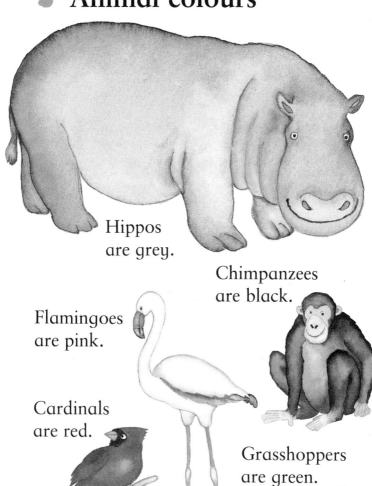

Hippos
are grey.

Chimpanzees
are black.

Flamingoes
are pink.

Cardinals
are red.

Grasshoppers
are green.

Lions are
golden.

Kingfishers
are blue.

Mice are
brown.

But chameleons
can change colour.

I'm painting whiskers
on my face.

Which
animal
am I?

Spots and stripes

Ladybirds have spots.

So do leopards.

Pandas have patches.

Giraffes have blotches.

Bees and wasps
have stripes.

bee

wasp

So do
zebras.

Tigers have
stripes too.

Butterfly fish
have spots
and stripes!

11

⚘ Feathers and fur, shells and scales

Cats are soft and furry.

Chicks are fluffy.

Pigs are bristly.

Goats are hairy.

Hedgehogs are prickly.

Slugs are slimy.

But fish are scaly.

So are snakes.

Crabs have shells.

What do these things feel like?

Heads...

Cockatoos have crests.

Deer have antlers.

Elephants have two tusks and a long trunk.

A rhinoceros has horns.

...and tails

Rabbits have fluffy tails.

Ponies have hairy tails.

Beavers have flat tails.

Pigs have curly tails.

But a manx cat has no tail at all.

15

❧ Eyes and ears

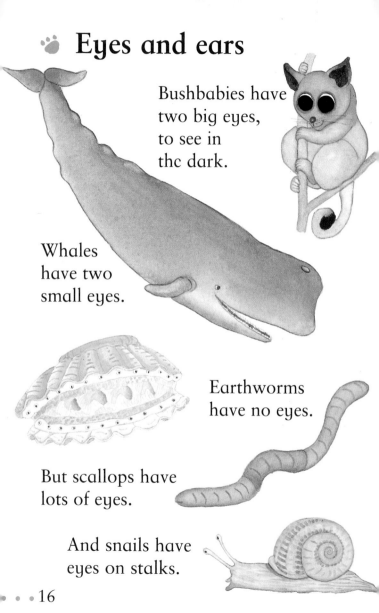

Bushbabies have
two big eyes,
to see in
the dark.

Whales
have two
small eyes.

Earthworms
have no eyes.

But scallops have
lots of eyes.

And snails have
eyes on stalks.

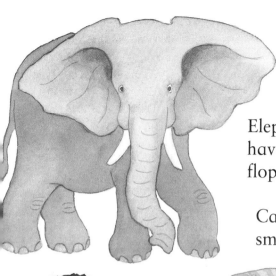

Elephants
have big
floppy ears.

Cats have
small ears.

Bears have
round ears.

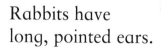

Rabbits have
long, pointed ears.

And crickets have ears
on their front legs.

🐾 Arms and legs

Watch out! The octopus has eight
long arms called tentacles.

Crabs have two
big claws.

Penguins
have flippers.

But dragonflies
have wings.

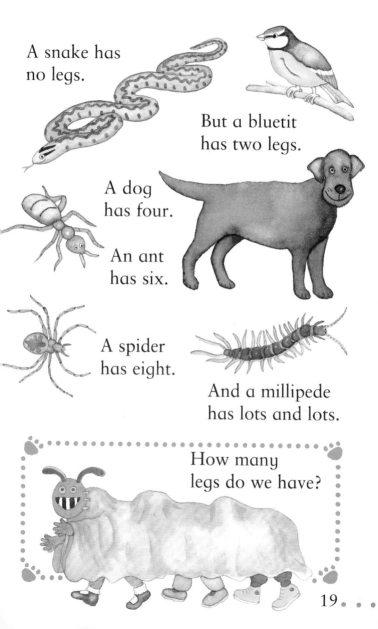

A snake has no legs.

But a bluetit has two legs.

A dog has four.

An ant has six.

A spider has eight.

And a millipede has lots and lots.

How many legs do we have?

19

Off we go!

Can you swim? Fish can swim.

Horses gallop.

Snakes slither.

Spiders creep.

Kittens pounce.

Frogs leap.

Tigers stalk.

Kangaroos bound.

Grasshoppers hop.

Which animals move like this?

Noisy animals

Dogs bark.

Kookaburras laugh.

Cats miaow.

Cows moo.

Pigs grunt.

Can you match the sounds to the animals?

OINK OINK

WOOF WOOF

MOO MOO

Frogs
croak.

Bees
buzz.

Snakes
hiss.

Owls
hoot.

Ducks quack.

Lions
ROAR!

TWIT
TWOO

hiss

23

Hungry animals

Munch, munch, what's for lunch?

Sheep nibble grass.

Koalas chew eucalyptus leaves.

Squirrels crunch nuts.

Gorillas gnaw fruit.

Caterpillars munch leaves.

Humming birds suck nectar.

But owls gulp mice.

Anteaters lick up termites.

And spiders gobble up flies.

I like melons!

What do you like to eat?

✿ Animal babies

kitten

puppy

chick

caterpillar

tadpole

cub

lamb

joey

calf

foal

Can you find the mother of each baby?

Animal mothers

butterfly

dog

sheep

cow

lioness

cat

penguin

horse

kangaroo

frog

27

ꙮ Time for bed

Squirrels
sleep in
a drey.

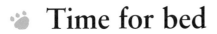

Beavers
sleep
in a
lodge.

Foxes
sleep in
a den.

Chimpanzees sleep in a nest.

Rabbits sleep in a warren.

Where do you like to sleep?